HUMANS IN SPACE

RETURN TO THE MOON

DAVID JEFFERIS AND MAT IRVINE

Crabtree Publishing Company

www.crabtreebooks.com

Introduction

Welcome to the Moon, and the future of human space flight. Astronauts first landed on the Moon in 1969, but none have gone back since the last mission in 1972. Now, more than 30 years later, the Moon is a target for human exploration once again. When will people return to the Moon? It's too soon to set an exact date but it is hoped that astronauts will be making regular flights there starting in the year 2015.

Pictures from above right, clockwise:
1   A boot print in dusty Moon soil.
2   A Saturn V rocket lifts off.
3   Buzz Aldrin, the second human on the Moon.
4   Future astronauts set up equipment.
5   The Moon's familiar face.

Crabtree Publishing Company
PMB 16A,
350 Fifth Avenue, Suite 3308
New York, NY 10118

616 Welland Avenue,
St. Catharines, Ontario
L2M 5V6

Coordinating Editor: Ellen Rodger
Project Editors: Carrie Gleason,
L. Michelle Nielsen
Production Coordinator: Rose Gowsell
Prepress technician: Nancy Johnson

Educational advisor:
Julie Stapleton
Written and produced by:
David Jefferis and Mat Irvine/Buzz Books

Library of Congress
Cataloging-in-Publication Data

Jefferis, David.
   Return to the moon / written by David Jefferis & Mat Irvine.
      p. cm. -- (Humans in space)
   Includes index.
   ISBN-13: 978-0-7787-3103-0 (rlb)
   ISBN-10: 0-7787-3103-0 (rlb)
   ISBN-13: 978-0-7787-3117-7 (pb)
   ISBN-10: 0-7787-3117-0 (pb)
   1. Moon--Juvenile literature. 2. Moon--Exploration--Juvenile literature.
   3. Satellites--Juvenile literature. I. Irvine, Mat. II. Title. III. Series.

QB582.J44 2007
523.3--dc22

2007003463

Contents

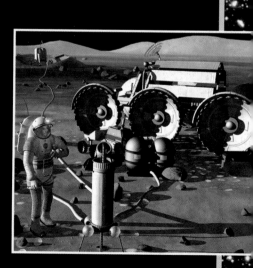

Earth's neighbor in space

The Moon may be our closest destination in space, but it is an utterly alien environment. Unlike Earth, the Moon has no air, no seas or oceans – and no life.

Take a look at the night sky. It's likely that the Moon is shining brightly, but the Moon has no light of its own. The Moon glows because it reflects sunlight toward Earth. There are many differences between the Earth and the Moon. An Earth day, or one rotation of the Earth, is 24 hours. The Moon rotates more slowly, so its "days" are longer. A day on the Moon lasts nearly an Earth-month, and is divided into two weeks of light and two weeks of darkness. The Moon is smaller than the Earth, and its **gravity** is only one-sixth as strong as that of the Earth.

▲ In the 1600s, early astronomers such as Galileo Galilei used simple instruments like these to sketch maps of the Moon.

Earth is covered with seas and oceans. The atmosphere **contains** the air people breathe and protects them from harmful rays from the Sun

The Moon shown to scale with Earth

Earth

▲ The Earth is 7,927 miles (12,756 kilometers) across. The Moon has a diameter of just 2,160 miles (3,476 kilometers), and is Earth's only natural **satellite**.

Where did the Moon come from?

There are several ideas as to how the Moon was created. Today, most scientists agree on the impact theory.

According to the impact theory, about 4.5 billion years ago a massive space object collided with Earth, splashing off vast quantities of the planet in the explosion. That material eventually joined together to form the Moon.

At about the same time, the Earth and the Moon were both bombarded with millions of space rocks, creating vast craters. We can still see these craters on the Moon's surface. On Earth, most of them have disappeared because of constant land and sea movements over millions of years.

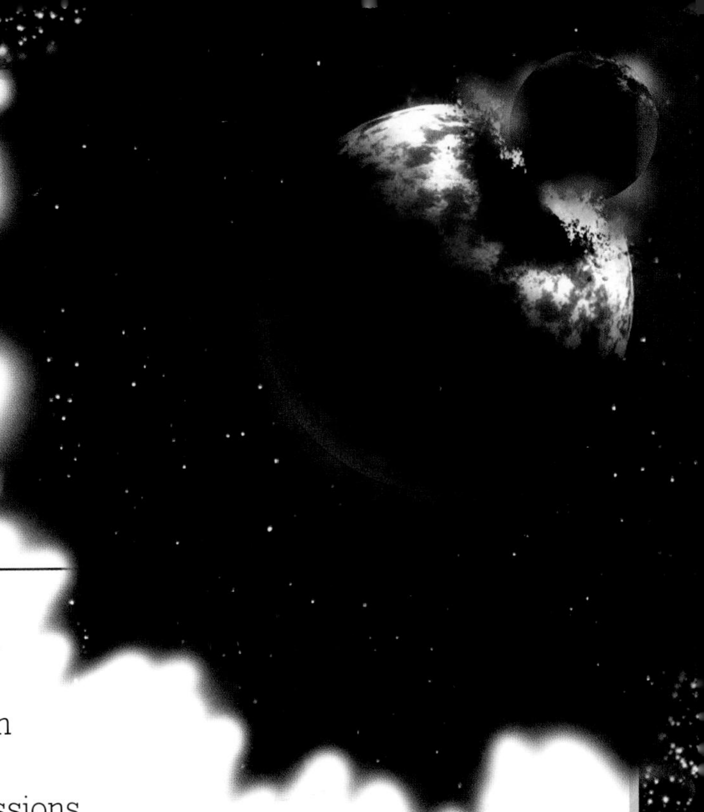

The Moon moves through space around the Earth in a near-circular path, or **orbit**, about 239,000 miles (384,000 kilometers) away. As distances here on Earth go, this is a very long way, but it is considered "next door" in space. **Apollo** astronauts, who flew missions to the Moon from 1969 to 1972, made the journey in about three days.

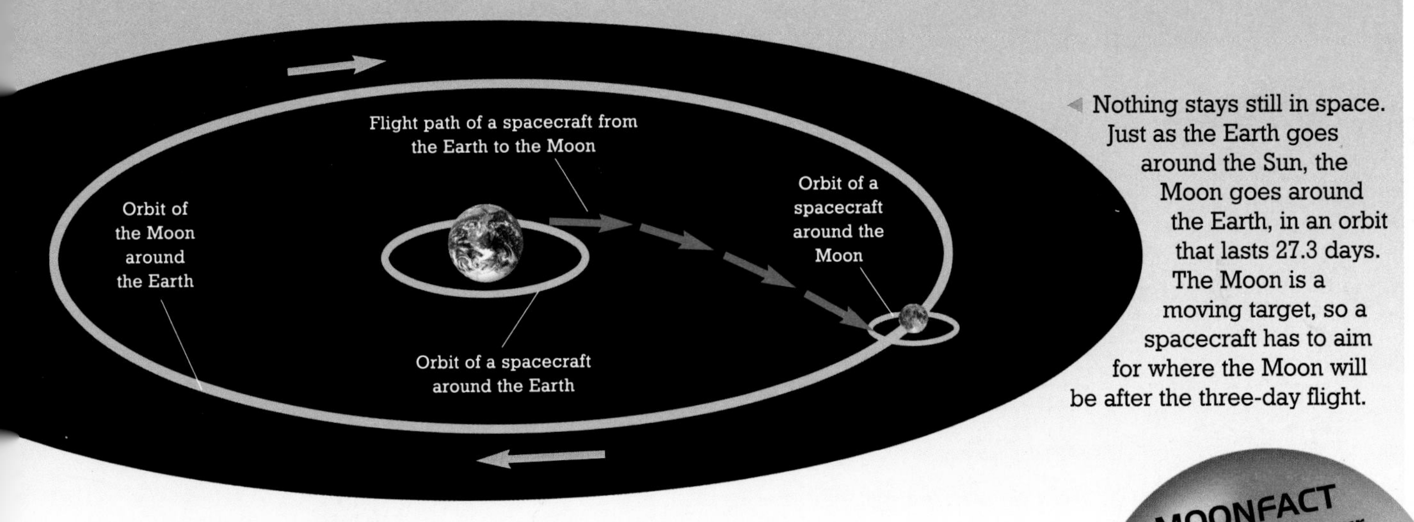

Orbit of the Moon around the Earth

Flight path of a spacecraft from the Earth to the Moon

Orbit of a spacecraft around the Earth

Orbit of a spacecraft around the Moon

◀ Nothing stays still in space. Just as the Earth goes around the Sun, the Moon goes around the Earth, in an orbit that lasts 27.3 days. The Moon is a moving target, so a spacecraft has to aim for where the Moon will be after the three-day flight.

Early astronomers thought the dark areas of the Moon were seas and oceans. In fact, they are vast, dry plains that were formed by the impact of huge rocks from space. The strongest hits were so violent that they cracked the Moon's surface like an eggshell. Molten, or melted, rock from inside the Moon bubbled up and flooded out to form dark spots.

▼ The Earth and Moon are shown here to scale for size and distance. In reality they are about 239,000 miles (384,000 kilometers) apart.

MOONFACT
We may think that our world's hot deserts and icy mountains give us extremes of temperature, but the Moon is much harsher. Daytime roasts at more than 248°F (120°C). At night, temperatures plunge to -274°F (-170°C) below freezing.

Moon

The Moon close-up

Before humans could visit the Moon, space probes **were sent to check that it was safe to land on the surface.**

Luna 9 unfolded four petal-shaped legs after landing. Once it was steady, the probe took pictures of the surface.

Throughout the 1960s, there was a race into space between the United States and the **Soviet Union**. The Soviet Union was made up of several states, the most powerful of which was Russia, still one of the major space powers.

Early on, the Soviet Union led the race. In 1966, its Luna 9 was the first space probe to touch down safely on the Moon's surface. The 218-pound (99-kilogram) probe confirmed that a controlled landing was possible, and took pictures of the rocks nearby.

▶ As the Moon circles the Earth, the same side always faces us. No one had ever seen the **far side** until 1959, when the Luna 3 space probe took this picture. This first glimpse showed the far side had many craters.

This "sky-sailing box" was thought up in 1650 and was meant to fly to the Moon

This Moon creature was drawn in about 1750

Science fiction space adventures

The idea of travel to the Moon dates back hundreds of years. Early stories were fantasies, with no practical ideas on how to build a real spacecraft.

Two writers who became famous for their space stories were Jules Verne from France, and Britain's H.G. Wells. Verne's 1865 book *From the Earth to the Moon* followed a group of explorers while they built a huge gun to shoot a capsule to the Moon. The spacecraft in Wells's 1901 book *The First Men in the Moon* was coated in a special material to shield it from the effects of gravity. It could float away from Earth without needing rockets!

Jules Verne   H.G. Wells

▼ **Lunar** Orbiter probes sent back detailed information about the Moon's surface. In 1966, this picture was the first to show an **earthrise**.

America was not far behind the Soviet Union. In 1966, the United States sent probes, called Lunar Orbiters, to the Moon. They took spectacular pictures but did not land. The U.S. Surveyor probes, which were built a few years later, touched down safely on the surface. Before this, no one knew exactly what conditions were like on the Moon. One theory said there was a layer of dust so deep that an entire spacecraft would sink into it!

▲ In November 1969, astronauts of the Apollo 12 mission landed near the Surveyor 3 probe, which had landed on the surface of the Moon in mid-1967.

The spacecraft from Verne's book was fired from a huge underground gun

H.G. Wells's football-shaped craft was covered with "cavorite," a fictional substance that allowed flight without needing rockets

Wells's explorers were captured by Selenites, beings that lived beneath the Moon's surface

In Verne's story, his explorers went to the Moon in a bullet-shaped capsule

The mighty Saturn

The first rocket to send humans to the Moon was the Saturn V. From its massive base to its slender tip, it towered more than 360 feet (110 meters) high.

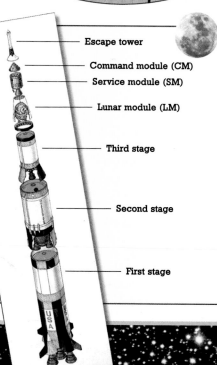

► The huge size of the Saturn V can be seen in this picture by comparing it to the size of the people standing next to it (circled). This picture shows a Saturn rocket being assembled.

▲ Saturn rockets were a part of **NASA's** Apollo program and were built inside the vast Vehicle Assembly Building (VAB). The VAB is still used for **Space Shuttle** missions.

The Saturn V was huge in every way. When fueled and loaded for flight, the great rocket weighed nearly 3,307 tons (3,000 tonnes). It was designed to lift an entire three-man Moon expedition, including the command **module** and Moon landing module.

Monster Moon rocket

The Saturn V (the "V" is the Roman numeral for 5) was built in a number of modules, or large sections, which joined together to form the whole spacecraft.

The three-man crew started their flight in the command module (CM). The escape tower could rocket them to safety in an emergency during takeoff, but luckily it was never needed. It dropped away soon after the rocket left the ground. The first and second **stages** also dropped away when their fuel was used up.

The CM and its attached service module (SM) linked to the lunar module (LM) in Earth orbit. These three sections went to the Moon, powered by the third stage. Only the LM landed on the Moon. The crew came back to Earth in the CM, which separated from the other modules, floating down to the ocean using three huge parachutes.

- Escape tower
- Command module (CM)
- Service module (SM)
- Lunar module (LM)
- Third stage
- Second stage
- First stage

▲ Apollo 11 leaves the launch
pad in July 1969 – the first crewed
mission to land on the Moon.

◄ The service tower enabled
technicians to check each part of
the Saturn rocket. The platforms
that swung out from the tower are
called service arms.

Saturn V had three
stages, or modules,
that had motors and fuel.
The first stage powered
the takeoff with five
rocket motors. Once this
stage had used up all its
fuel, it dropped away and
the smaller second stage
took over. A final push
from Earth to Moon was
given by the third stage.

The only part of the
Saturn V to return to
Earth was the command
module. It separated
from the service module
before entering the
Earth's atmosphere.

Humans on the Moon

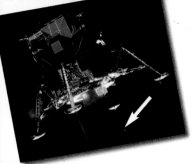

The Apollo missions to the Moon were not meant to be long-stay explorations. The crew of the first landing flight, Apollo 11, stayed on the surface less than 22 hours.

Various parts of the Saturn rocket were left behind as fuel was used up. The only parts of the spacecraft to go around the Moon were the command and service modules (CSM), attached to the lunar module (LM). Two of the three crew from Apollo 11 climbed into the LM, while the third, Michael Collins, stayed behind in the CSM.

▲ The *Eagle* was Apollo 11's lunar module. Stick-like probes (arrowed) switched on an instrument panel light when they touched the Moon's surface.

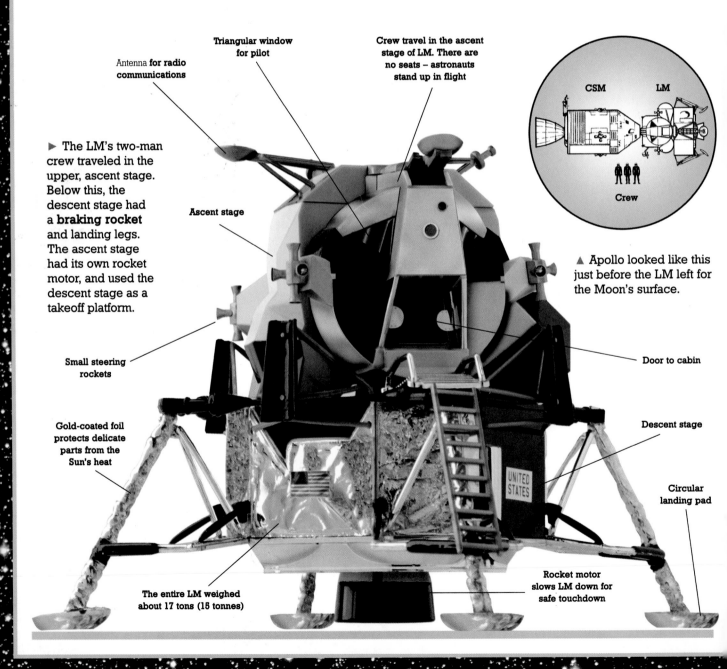

Triangular window for pilot

Crew travel in the ascent stage of LM. There are no seats – astronauts stand up in flight

Antenna **for radio communications**

▶ The LM's two-man crew traveled in the upper, ascent stage. Below this, the descent stage had a **braking rocket** and landing legs. The ascent stage had its own rocket motor, and used the descent stage as a takeoff platform.

Ascent stage

CSM   LM

Crew

▲ Apollo looked like this just before the LM left for the Moon's surface.

Small steering rockets

Door to cabin

Gold-coated foil protects delicate parts from the Sun's heat

Descent stage

UNITED STATES

Circular landing pad

The entire LM weighed about 17 tons (15 tonnes)

Rocket motor slows LM down for safe touchdown

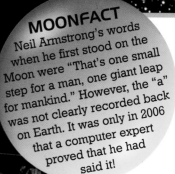

◄ Apollo 11 astronaut Buzz Aldrin stands by a device that measured particles from the Sun. The space suits did not bend much at the knees, so astronauts found it easier to move in gentle hops and leaps.

Flying the LM on Apollo 11 were Neil Armstrong and Buzz Aldrin. Before undocking from the command module, they powered up the LM, extended its landing legs and checked all the systems. These jobs took more than four hours.

Once under way, the two astronauts flew feet first toward the Moon's surface. Their speed was controlled by the braking rocket under the LM's descent stage. Armstrong piloted the LM while Aldrin called off the height readings. Then, on July 20, 1969, the craft finally settled onto the surface. In Armstrong's famous words, "The *Eagle* has landed."

"Danger – there are big rocks down there!"

The first Moon landing was in grave danger, when Neil Armstrong reported that they were "running long," or heading west of the intended site. The spacecraft computer was taking them toward an area covered with big rocks around a crater. Armstrong took over flight control and, helped by guidance from crewmate Buzz Aldrin, flew the lunar module down to a safe landing – with less than 30 seconds' worth of fuel left in the tank! The landing site was named Tranquility Base, after the Sea of Tranquility, the part of the Moon they landed on.

This blurry television image was all people on Earth could see when Armstrong set foot on the Moon

Driving on the Moon

Exploring on foot meant that Apollo astronauts stayed near the lunar module. To travel further, an electric-powered lunar roving vehicle (LRV) was developed.

The first humans to drive on the Moon were Apollo 15 astronauts David Scott and James Irwin. They used a lunar roving vehicle to explore a part of the Moon called Hadley Rille in July 1971. The LRV was carried on the side of the lunar module, folded up into a neat package about the size of a baby's playpen. Scott and Irwin simply unfolded the LRV when they were ready to drive it.

▲ The **Lunokhod** 1 robot Moon **rover** was launched in 1970 by the Soviet Union. It took more than 20,000 TV pictures.

▼ The last two Apollo missions also carried an LRV. Here, Apollo 17 astronaut Harrison Schmitt pauses by a massive boulder, as he takes samples of Moon rock in December 1972. This was the last Apollo flight and, at just under 75 hours, the longest stay on the Moon.

The LRV had an electric motor in each wheel. The two-seater Moon buggy could travel on the dusty lunar soil at up to ten miles per hour (16 kilometers per hour) on level ground.

MOONFACT
The LRV was developed very quickly – the design team took it from sketchpad to a working machine in just 17 months. The rover was full of simple but good ideas, such as a navigation aid that used the Sun's shadow to show direction.

What will a future rover look like?

The Apollo LRV was a great success, and future rovers will probably not look too different. The design shown (right) is one idea for such a vehicle. It has six big wheels to travel easily over rough ground, with a set of wheelguards to prevent dust from being thrown up on the two astronauts sitting onboard.

Power for the vehicle comes from a set of heavy-duty batteries. Each of the six wheels has an electric motor in the hub. This is a safety feature – up to three motors could break down before the rover would come to a halt.

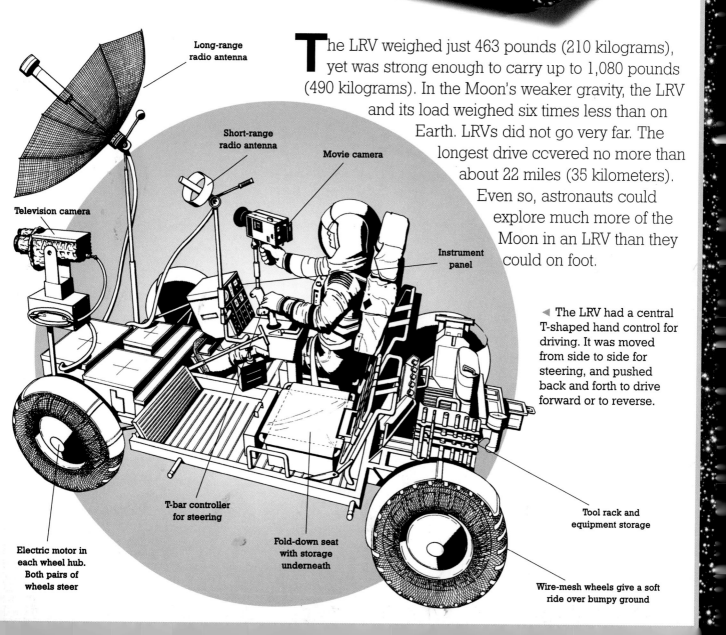

The LRV weighed just 463 pounds (210 kilograms), yet was strong enough to carry up to 1,080 pounds (490 kilograms). In the Moon's weaker gravity, the LRV and its load weighed six times less than on Earth. LRVs did not go very far. The longest drive covered no more than about 22 miles (35 kilometers). Even so, astronauts could explore much more of the Moon in an LRV than they could on foot.

◄ The LRV had a central T-shaped hand control for driving. It was moved from side to side for steering, and pushed back and forth to drive forward or to reverse.

Long-range radio antenna

Short-range radio antenna

Movie camera

Television camera

Instrument panel

T-bar controller for steering

Fold-down seat with storage underneath

Electric motor in each wheel hub. Both pairs of wheels steer

Tool rack and equipment storage

Wire-mesh wheels give a soft ride over bumpy ground

Moon science

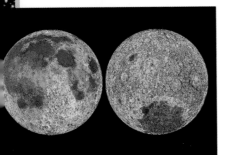

During their stays on the Moon, the Apollo astronauts carried out scientific research.

▲ These are geological maps of the Moon. Blue areas show the lowest land areas, red the highest, and green in between.

The goal of the Apollo program was to get humans on the Moon before the Soviet Union did. There was also a lot to find out about the Moon. Astronauts carried out many science experiments. Collecting rocks and soil samples was a top priority. Only a few minutes after Armstrong's first steps on the Moon, he was scooping up samples for the scientists back on Earth who were eagerly waiting to inspect them.

No one knew if there was life on the Moon. It was thought unlikely but, just in case, astronauts and soil samples went into sealed chambers on their return to Earth. Rock tests included grinding some to dust. The dust was placed with plants and animals to see if they caught any diseases from alien "bugs" brought back from the Moon.

▲ Apollo 16 astronaut Charles Duke works by a LRV. The big antenna is part of the LRV, not Duke's space helmet!

HORNET + 3

◀ The crews of Apollo 11, 12, and 14 were sealed off for a time. No Moon life was found, so later Apollo crews did not have to do this.

cience experiments included placing a
square **retro reflector** on the Moon in 1969.
The device, which is still in use, has a group of
mirrors that reflect powerful **laser** light beams
flashed from Earth. By measuring the time
taken for the reflection to return to Earth,
scientists work out the distance between
the two places. The equipment has also
shown that the Moon is moving slowly
away from the Earth, at a rate of just
1.5 inches (38 millimeters) a year.

◀ Taking samples of Moon soil was important
work. Here James Irwin scoops out a shallow
hole with a tool specially made for the job.

Was it all a hoax?

Some people have claimed that the Apollo flights
were faked to trick the world into thinking the United
States had beaten the Soviet Union to the Moon.
These people say that the flights were a hoax and
the photographs were faked.

Anyone who saw a Saturn V thunder into the sky
would argue against the "hoax" theory. What hoax
believers believe are "technical errors" in pictures
of the Apollo missions have been explained by
professional photographers.

It was probably easier to really go to the Moon,
than to bribe the thousands of people who worked
on the Apollo program to lie about it!

The Apollo retro reflector still works. It
was placed on the Moon by Armstrong and
Aldrin in 1969

Return to the Moon

At last, the Moon is once again a target for human exploration. The next crewed missions could be flying there as early as 2015.

▲ The crew module of the new spacecraft is called the **Orion**. It looks similar to the old Apollo command module, but is bigger, with room for up to six people.

Plans for future spacecraft launches to the Moon include using two smaller rockets instead of the mighty Saturn V. A trip to the Moon will begin with the **Ares** V cargo rocket lifting a lunar **lander**, called the **Artemis**, into Earth orbit. A smaller rocket, called the Ares I, will then lift the crew into space.

▼ **Booster** rockets and cargo nose sections fall away, as the Ares V leaves the Earth behind. Carried at the nose is a four-person lunar landing vehicle.

◄ The Orion will be able to **dock** with the **International Space Station, (ISS)** taking over supply jobs from the present-day Space Shuttle.

The Ares V boosters burn solid fuel, much like giant firework rockets

The main rocket motors are based on the design of those used on the Saturn V

First stage fuel tank

The crew will travel in an Orion spaceship. This will look much like the old Apollo command module, but will have room inside for up to six people. For Moon trips, however, plans allow for just four astronauts to make the trip. Once in Earth orbit, the Orion will dock with the Artemis lunar lander.

Ares V upper stage powers the mission from Earth orbit to the Moon

Fuel tanks for the Artemis descent stage

Artemis ascent stage carries up to four people

A rocket they call "the stick"

The Ares I and Ares V rockets are fairly simple designs. They will replace the very complex Space Shuttle system when it is retired in about 2010.

The pencil-slim Ares I is nicknamed "the stick." The Orion crew module has no Shuttle-type wings. Instead, parachutes will be used for landing. Some details are carried over from the Space Shuttle, such as the two booster rockets of the Ares V.

Ares I crew-carrier rocket, named "the stick"

Ares V cargo-carrier rocket

When the Orion and Artemis are safely linked together and fully checked, the next step will be to leave Earth orbit behind and set off on the three-day flight to Moon orbit.

Nose sections protect cargo as the rocket flies through Earth's atmosphere. Once in space, these sections fall away

MOONFACT
The *Orion* looks similar to an Apollo module, but it is much improved, with new materials and electronics. Comfort features will include a small camping-style toilet and a unisex "relief tube," far easier to use than the plastic bags used before.

Space voyage

▲ The Orion crew module joins to the Artemis lunar lander, and then the Ares V upper stage thrusts them from Earth orbit (1), toward the Moon.

▼ Artemis descends to the Moon (5), leaving the Orion to orbit the Moon with no one aboard. After landing (6), the four astronauts set up their equipment, including a rover. Space suits may be colored (7) for easy recognition.

The flight from Earth to the Moon takes about three days, and is a trip that has not been made for many years. Here is a step-by-step look at a future mission.

The Orion crew will travel backwards for much of the trip, because their craft will be docked back-to-front with the Artemis lunar lander. Once the Ares V upper stage has increased enough speed to escape from Earth orbit, it will shut off. The expedition will then coast through space until braking rockets slow it down to enter orbit around the Moon.

Chefs have a lot of experience making food for the International Space Station (2, 3) so Orion crews should eat well. After the three-day flight, Orion and Artemis go into orbit around the Moon (4).

Safely in Moon orbit, the four astronauts will climb into the Artemis and set off for a surface mission of a week or more. To return to the Orion module, they will blast off in the Artemis. After redocking with the Orion and climbing inside, they will fire up its motor to return home to Earth.

Once in the Earth's upper atmosphere, parachutes will slow the Orion to a safe speed, and **airbags** will pop out to give a soft landing on the ground.

Tasty space snacks

In-flight food has come a long way since the early days of space flight when astronauts had to suck glop from squeeze tubes or chew dried food that came in bite-sized cubes.

Today's astronauts eat with a knife, fork, and spoon from trays that stop food from floating away. However, most food is precooked on Earth. The only fresh items are fruit and vegetables, which are stored in lockers. Some items keep better in space than others. Carrots and celery rot in a couple of days.

Wherever they come from, astronauts love to eat some familiar foods. South Korean food experts are working on a space-friendly version of kimchi, a spicy and popular vegetable dish!

▶ When the Orion returns to Earth, it floats to the ground under huge parachutes (8). Airbags pop out (9) to cushion the landing.

MOONFACT
The Orion will be reusable after a Moon flight. Orions are being designed to make up to ten trips. It will be possible to reuse an Orion because it will land on the ground, not in the sea. Salt ___ges delicate

Staying on the Moon

▲ A single-seat rocket chair could make a quick way of getting around on the Moon.

Future Moon missions could last from a week to a month or more. A chief goal will be learning to live safely on a world with no air – dangerous, but possible.

▲ This is another possible lunar lander design with the square body making it an efficient carrier. In the distance sits a cargo ship from Earth.

Apollo expeditions on the Moon lasted three days at most. The crews did not get much sleep in their lunar modules. There were no beds, and the floor was the only place that astronauts could lie down to get some rest. On future trips astronauts will stay for at least a week. The goal is to remain on the Moon for even longer, so comfortable living conditions will be important. Astronauts will have access to more equipment, including cooking tools, sleeping bags, and even foam mats to lie on.

▶ Robots of various kinds will be essential equipment on future Moon missions. Here an astronaut makes some adjustments to a rock-sampling rover.

The robotic arm is used for inspecting rocks and placing them in the trailer

A trailer carries rock samples back to the base

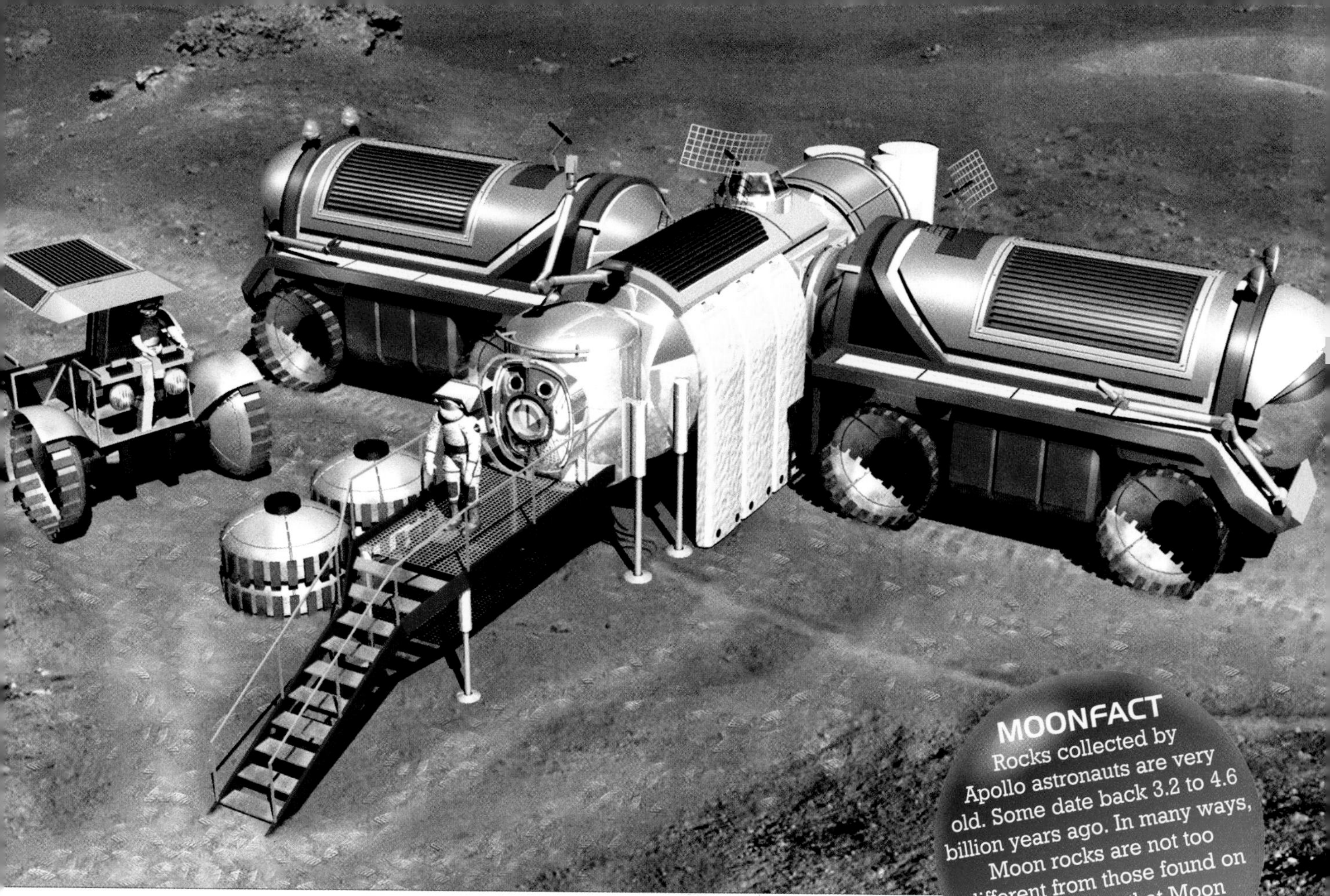

▲ A small rover is used for local trips near the base.

Plans for future Moon expeditions are not yet fixed, but could include a base like the one above. This picture shows truck-size rovers backing up to a center module, which stays fixed in place. The rovers are meant to go on research trips. They dock at the center module when they return. The module has a laboratory, storage, and communications equipment.

International competition heats up

Returning to the Moon is now an international goal. Several countries, especially Russia, China, and India are keen to send spacecraft, though not all will have humans aboard.

Russia's plans are among the most advanced, with its rocket-maker, the Energia Corporation, designing a new spacecraft called the Kliper.

The six-seater Kliper will be able to take off from a Russian launch base or the European space center in French Guiana, a territory in South America.

Kliper will look like a chunky jet plane. Its wings will let it fly through the Earth's atmosphere when returning to base. The first flights will be to the International Space Station, but there are plans to make a round-the-Moon Kliper flight in 2011-2012.

Later still, a Kliper might be used for the much longer flight to the distant red planet, Mars.

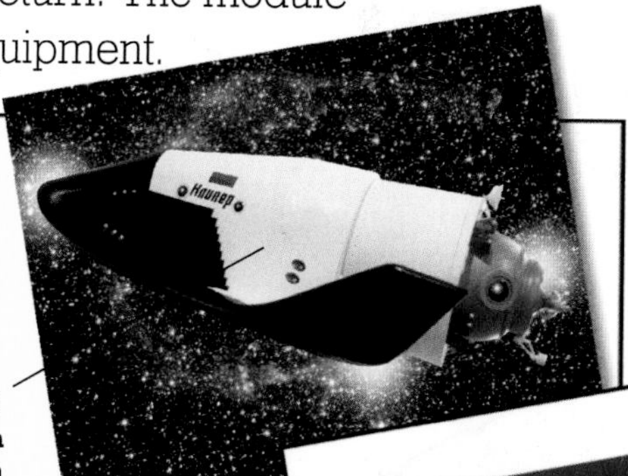

Russia's Kliper spacecraft will carry a two-person crew, and up to four passengers

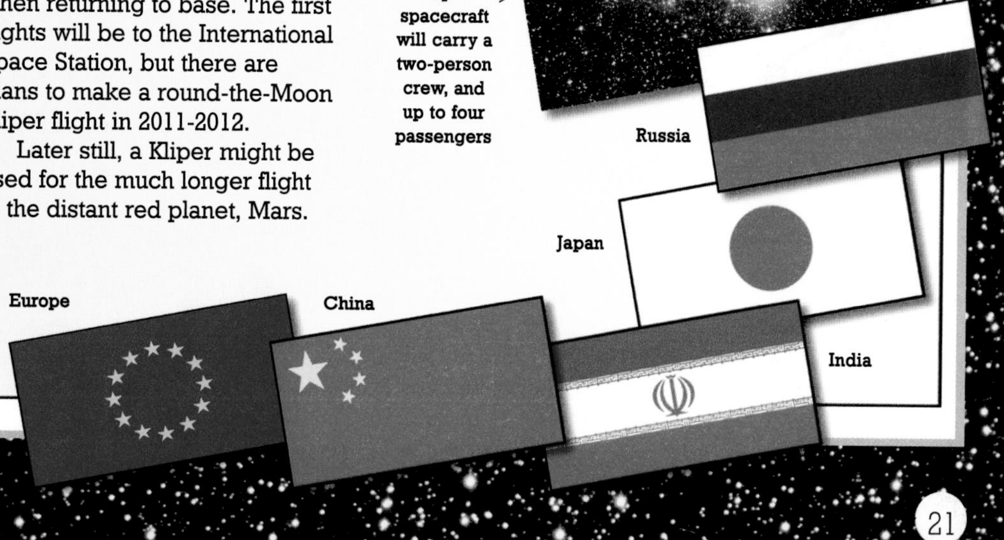

Russia

Japan

Europe

China

India

Moon miners

One day the Moon may be mined for its minerals, **and perhaps for water, in the form of ice, hidden in deep craters.**

Moon explorers in the future will be trying to find what resources lie there. Already space probes have looked for ice in the shadowed parts of craters near the Moon's polar regions, where the Sun's rays never shine. Scientists think that up to 331 million tons (300 million tonnes) of water could be frozen in the soil.

▲ Lunar Prospector (top) is a probe built to hunt for ice in craters near the Moon's North and South Poles (arrowed).

Finding a large source of water could change the Moon from a gray wasteland into a **colony** that can support astronauts. It would be easier and cheaper to use water from the Moon than having to haul it all the way from Earth.

▶ The far side of the Moon would be a good place for astronauts to put powerful telescopes to view distant space objects.

▲ Astronauts check their mining instruments while surveying during the long lunar night.

◀ A **geologist** prepares a drill to take rock samples from deep under the Moon's surface. Her helmet light is needed for work during the very long, two-week lunar night.

Another possible use for the Moon is as a huge observatory. The Moon has no atmosphere, so there would be no blurry telescope images from dust, pollution, or shifting air currents like on Earth. The far side always faces away from Earth, so it is protected from the electronic interference caused by radio and television signals. Instruments could be placed on the far side to investigate distant stars and galaxies, without being disturbed.

Is the Moon's low gravity dangerous?

The light gravity of the Moon makes some things easy, such as lifting heavy weights, but low gravity holds risks for humans. On long stays, without Earth's strong gravity pull, the body's natural systems get "lazy." **Calcium** goes out of the bones, the heart does not have to pump so hard, and muscles waste away. When astronauts return to Earth, they are weak, but begin to recover their strength after a while.

At present experts say that one-quarter gravity pull, which is more than the Moon's, could be needed to keep the body working properly. This cannot be proven until people have stayed on the Moon for at least six months.

MOONFACT
The long nights on the Moon may cause problems for some types of work. Nights last two weeks, so astronauts at work will need powerful lights. The Apollo flights were timed so that landings were made during the Moon's two weeks of light.

Like all astronauts staying on the International Space Station, astronaut Frank Culbertson Jr. has to exercise regularly on the running machine and other fitness equipment

Future Moon base

If valuable minerals are found on the Moon one day, then a permanent base or even an entire colony could be built there.

▲ This Moon base was drawn for a science fiction story in an *Eagle* comic in 1958, and showed how things might look one day. The story was ahead of its time. A base like this still lies about 50 years in the future.

Just suppose the Moon has valuable minerals as well as a source of water. If they are cheaper and easier to mine than on Earth, operations on the Moon would be transformed. Instead of going there only for scientific interest, expeditions would go to make money, which means colonies could be set up.

▲ Complex entrances are needed on an airless world.

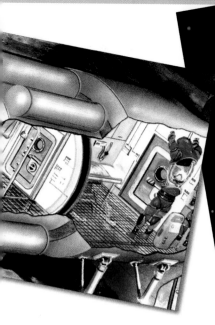

Inside the dome,
conditions would be
very comfortable

Main entrance to
"Crater City"

▲ This far-in-the-future
environment could be made
by covering a crater with a
clear dome, then filling it with
air and water.

Riches from the soil

This vision of a busy Moon town could come true by 2030 if the dreams of today's experts turn out to be correct.

The Moon's soil is thought to contain large amounts of a substance called **helium-3**, which is very rare on Earth. Helium-3 is important, because it could be used as a fuel for future power stations, creating very little pollution or dangerous waste.

There are other useful things in lunar soil, such as oxygen. Oxygen is shown here being mined for rocket fuel. It is far easier to send crafts into space from the Moon than the Earth, because the Moon's gravity is weaker. One day, this could turn the Moon into a huge "fuel stop" in the sky, and an important launch pad for spaceflight to more distant places.

Living on the Moon will never be easy. Conditions there are very dangerous. Any future base will need to have its living areas underground, for protection against the Sun's rays and the lack of air on the surface. Oxygen could be made from the soil, and the two weeks of light should make it possible to grow plenty of nourishing crops in greenhouses. One day, some astronauts may decide to stay permanently on the Moon, perhaps even raising families there.

MOONFACT
If children are born on the Moon, it is unlikely that they could visit Earth without booster drugs and support equipment. Life in just one-sixth gravity will almost certainly result in a weaker heart and muscles than those of an Earth-born human.

I/o 2/o 3/1 4/2

5/63+

Other moons

The worlds circling the Sun have more than 150 moons between them. Will humans explore any of them in the future? New and improved space technology will be needed for this to happen.

There is one huge difference between going to Earth's Moon, and visiting one circling another planet – distance. A mission to the Moon involves a journey time of about three days each way, but the other planets and their moons are much further away. For example, a flight to Mars will take at least six months. Apart from the time involved, the dangers of deep-space flights include equipment breakdowns and deadly particles emitted from the Sun when storms and flares break out on its surface.

▼ Triton is a frozen moon of Neptune, far away from the Sun.

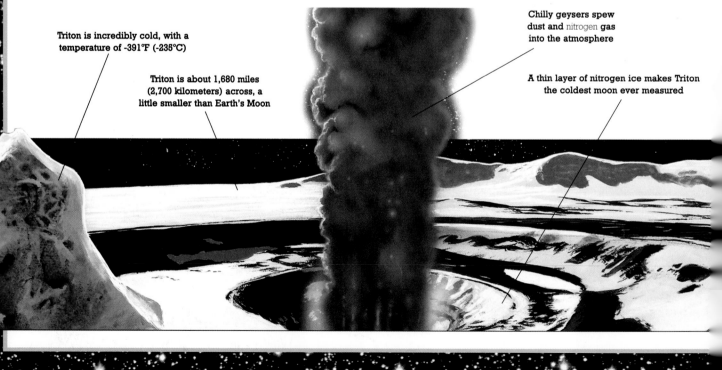

Triton is incredibly cold, with a temperature of -391°F (-235°C)

Triton is about 1,680 miles (2,700 kilometers) across, a little smaller than Earth's Moon

Chilly geysers spew dust and nitrogen gas into the atmosphere

A thin layer of nitrogen ice makes Triton the coldest moon ever measured

◄ The major planets are shown here to scale. The yellow numbers show the number of moons so far discovered.
1   Mercury
2   Venus
3   Earth
4   Mars
5   Jupiter
6   Saturn
7   Uranus
8   Neptune

For the foreseeable future, humans will probably travel only in Earth orbit, to the Moon, and perhaps to the planet Mars and its pair of small, potato-shaped moons, called Phobos and Deimos.

To go further into space, new and much faster spacecrafts will need to be developed.

◄ The Earth and Moon are compared here with a part of the huge planet of Jupiter (left) and four of its biggest moons.

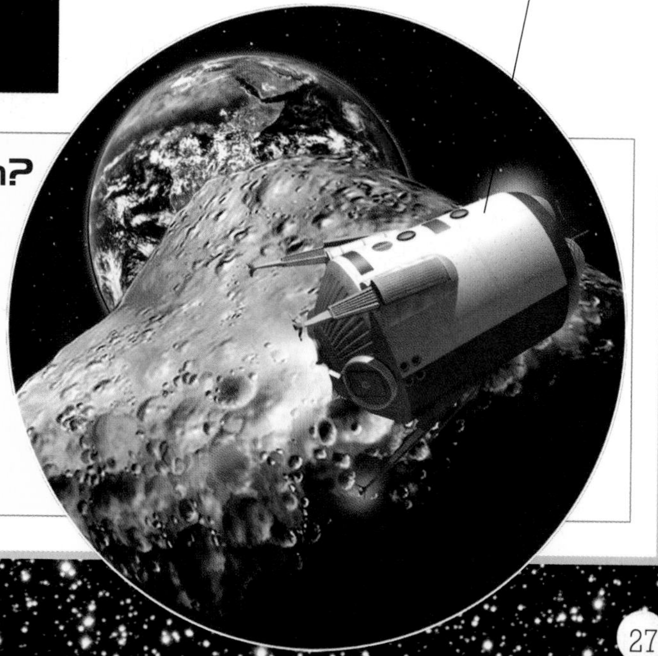

A future crewed spacecraft explores Cruithne

Does Earth have a second moon?

In 1986 scientists thought they had found a "second moon" orbiting Earth, which they called Cruithne. Cruithne is only three miles (five kilometers) long, and is not really a moon of Earth at all, but is an **asteroid** that shares Earth's orbit around the Sun.

It does not follow the exact same path as Earth. Instead, it travels far away before returning in its orbit closer to Earth. Cruithne is no danger to Moon-bound astronauts. The closest it gets to Earth is still about 30 times further away than the Moon.

Timeline

Here are discoveries and achievements marking journeys to the Moon – from ideas of the past to predictions of the future.

▲ Wernher von Braun was in charge of the Apollo program.

▲ A movie made in the early days of cinema by Georges Méliès featured a spacecraft crashing into the "face" of the Man in the Moon!

About 3000 B.C. Rock carvings at Knowth, Ireland, may show the Moon, making them the earliest human-made images of the Moon discovered so far.

About 500 B.C. Greek philosopher Anaxagoras reasons that the Moon is a giant spherical rock, and that it reflects the light of the Sun.

About 150 A.D. The Greek Lucian of Samosata writes *Vera Historia* (True History), probably the first story of a trip from the Earth to the Moon. Lucian tells of a ship that is lifted on a giant waterspout. The crew arrive during a war between the kings of the Moon and the Sun.

1200-1500 A.D. Even before the telescope is invented, many people agree that the Moon is a sphere. Despite its markings, they mostly think that the Moon's surface is smooth.

1609 The Italian astronomer Galileo Galilei looks at the Moon through the newly invented telescope. He makes one of the earliest drawings of it, and says that the Moon's markings show that it has mountains and craters.

1651 A detailed atlas of the Moon is produced by Italian astronomer Giovanni Riccioli. Many of the names he gives the Moon's features are still used today. Riccioli decides that the Moon is a dead, dry world, stating above his map, "No Man Dwell on the Moon."

1783 The first hot-air and gas-filled balloon flights are made. As flights go higher, it becomes clear that humans cannot survive far above the ground without breathing gear and other protection. Until these flights, it was thought that Earth's air went all the way to the Moon.

1865 French writer Jules Verne writes *From the Earth to the Moon* in which a space capsule is shot into space by a giant cannon.

1901 British author H.G. Wells publishes *The First Men in the Moon* in which explorers are captured by creatures living under the Moon's surface.

1957 The world's first space satellite is launched in October by the Soviet Union. Called Sputnik 1, it weighs 184 pounds (83.6 kilograms) and orbits the Earth once every 96 minutes.

1959 The first of a series of Soviet Moon probes is launched. In January, Luna 1 goes near the Moon, 3,725 miles (5,995 kilometers) away. In September, Luna 2 hits the Moon. In October, Luna 3 photographs the far side of the Moon.

1960 German scientist Wernher von Braun is placed in charge of U.S. space rocket development.

1961 Yuri Gagarin, from the Soviet Union, becomes the first human in space. He makes a single orbit of the Earth in the spacecraft Vostok 1.

1961 U.S. President John F. Kennedy declares the goal of landing a human on the Moon "by the end of the decade."

1965 Cosmonaut, or Russian astronaut, Aleksei Leonov carries out the first space walk, lasting 20 minutes outside the spacecraft Voskhod 2.

▼ An engineer adjusts a test model of the Apollo escape tower, an essential part of the safety systems of the huge Saturn V rocket.

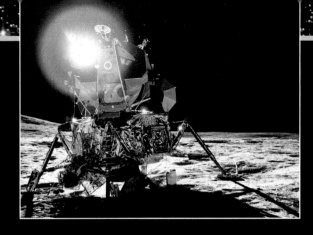

◄ Apollo 14's LM shows its gold foil covering, used to reflect the heat of the Sun's rays.

1966 Luna 9 makes a controlled soft landing on the Moon in January and takes pictures of the surface nearby. Later in the year, the first U.S. Lunar Orbiter probe starts mapping the Moon.

1966 U.S. spacecraft Gemini 8 makes the first docking with another spacecraft, an uncrewed Agena target vehicle.

1968 The first humans to leave Earth orbit fly in Apollo 8. The flight is not a landing mission. After orbiting the Moon, they return to Earth.

1969 The Apollo 9 flight in March tests all the Apollo hardware, including the lunar module (LM). For ten days, astronauts check the craft in Earth orbit, undocking and then redocking the LM with the command module. The flight is successful, allowing a Moon landing flight to go ahead in July.

1969 On July 20, astronauts Neil Armstrong and Buzz Aldrin become the first humans to set foot on the Moon, as they step outside their Apollo 11 lunar module.

1969-1972 Apollo 11 is followed by successful landings by Apollo 12, 14, 15, 16, and 17. The Apollo 13 mission suffered an explosion in the service module, which lost its oxygen and electrical supply. The crew managed to use their LM's supplies as a "space lifeboat" and were able to return safely to Earth.

1971 First use of a lunar roving vehicle (LRV) by the crew of Apollo 15.

2004 Long-term human spaceflight goals are announced for the U.S. space agency, NASA. They include plans to land on the Moon again some time between 2015 and 2020. Human flights to Mars, building on experience gained on the Moon, could start some time after this.

2006 Russia announces that its Kliper spacecraft could be making orbital flights around the Moon by 2012.

2010 The Ares I and Ares V rockets will start to replace the U.S. Space Shuttle. They will be used for American crewed missions into Earth orbit, and for preparing for a return to the Moon.

2012 Plans for Moon-return flights will be at a detailed stage.

2015 New landings will be made on the Moon.

2020 The first permanent Moon base could be set up, opening the way for colonies and humans living on the Moon.

2030 Several countries will make crewed Moon flights, including Russia, China, and India.

◄ Neil Armstrong checks the electronic systems in the Apollo 11 Landing Module. The black-and-white cap held earphones and a microphone. It was nicknamed the "Snoopy cap" because it looked like the famous cartoon dog's head!

► A future Moon base with inflatable domes would provide a comfortable living environment for explorers. The blue panels are solar panels, which provide power by making electricity from sunlight.

Glossary

The glossary provides explanations for some of the terms used in this book.

▲ A Russian spacecraft displays its docking port (arrowed).

▲ Large dish antennas are used to communicate with space missions to the Moon.

Airbag A balloon-like rubber and plastic bag that inflates to cushion an impact.

Antenna A rod or dish-shaped aerial that transmits or receives radio and TV signals.

Apollo The NASA space program that took humans to the Moon from 1969 to 1972. Apollo was named after the Ancient Greek and Roman god of all wisdom.

Ares The two rockets being developed for the new U.S. Moon program, named after the Greek god of war.

Artemis The U.S. four-person lunar module being developed for future missions, and named after the Greek goddess of hunting and the Moon.

Asteroid A rock-like object that orbits around the Sun and can be between 33 feet (ten meters) and 621 miles (1,000 kilometers) in size.

Atmosphere The blanket of gases that surrounds many planets. Earth's atmosphere is a mixture of mostly nitrogen and oxygen.

Booster An extra rocket that increases the lifting abilities of the main rocket at takeoff. Boosters drop away when their fuel is used up, usually only a minute or two after takeoff.

Braking rocket Any rocket motor that is used to slow down a spacecraft.

Calcium An essential element for healthy growth and upkeep of bones and teeth. Calcium is found in milk, cheese, nuts, beans, and many other foods.

Colony A territory settled by a group of people.

Dock Describes two spacecraft linking together. A docking port allows cargo and astronauts to move safely between two docked spacecraft.

Earthrise The rising of the Earth as viewed from a location on the Moon.

Far side The side of the Moon that always faces away from Earth. The "near side" is what we see.

Geologist A person who studies the physical make-up of Earth and other space bodies.

Gravity The force of attraction between objects. Massive objects have a stronger gravitational pull than less massive ones. Places with almost no gravity are said to have microgravity, or weightlessness.

Helium-3 A rare substance, thought to exist in Moon soil, that could be used as a clean fuel for a future form of power.

International Space Station (ISS) A crewed research base being built in Earth orbit. It is a project between the U.S., Russia, Japan, Canada, and Europe, plus many smaller contributors.

Lander A spacecraft built to make contact with the surface of a space object. A "hard" lander is made to crash into the ground; a "soft" lander takes down an instrument, package, or other load gently.

Laser A very strong pencil-thin beam of light. Scientists check the distance between Earth and the Moon by flashing a laser at the mirrors of a retro reflector, and timing how long it takes for the laser to be reflected back to Earth.

Lunar Anything relating to the Moon. "Luna" comes from the Latin name for the Moon.

Lunokhod The name, meaning "Moon Walker," given to a type of Russian-built robot lunar rover.

Minerals A natural substance, such as coal or salt, that is useful to people on Earth.

Module A section of a spacecraft. Examples are crew, cargo, or communications modules.

National Aeronautics and Space Administration (NASA) The United States' space agency.

Nitrogen A chemical substance that exists as a solid, liquid, or gas. Nitrogen gas makes up most of the Earth's atmosphere.

Orbit The curving path one space object takes around another.

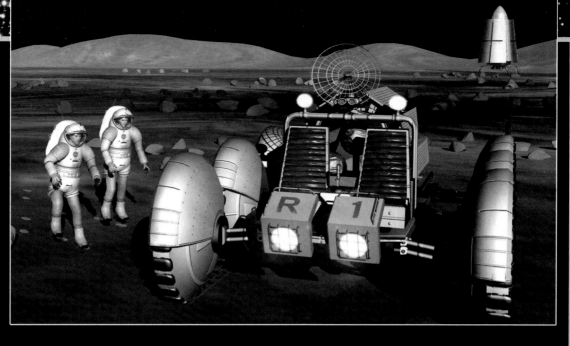

► Future lunar rovers could look similar to this design. It has very large wheels for driving across rough ground. Powerful lights allow astronauts to drive the rover in the two-week lunar night.

Orion The command module that will replace the U.S. Space Shuttle after about 2010. Orion was named after a giant hunter in Ancient Greek stories.

Oxygen A common chemical element found in rocks and as a gas in the air we breathe.

Retro reflector An instrument left on the Moon by the crew of Apollo 11 in 1969. It holds mirrors to reflect light back to Earth. The reflector's full name is the laser ranging retro reflector (LRRR).

Rover, roving vehicle A vehicle that moves on another world, driven by humans or guided by computers.

Satellite A space object that orbits another. The Moon is Earth's natural satellite, but there are thousands of human-made artificial satellites.

Soviet Union A group of 15 states, including Russia, that existed in Eastern Europe and Asia. From 1945 until 1991 the Soviet Union was one of the world's two superpowers, along with the United States. The Soviet Union collapsed in 1991, and the 15 states are now separate countries.

Space probe An uncrewed spacecraft sent to explore and record information about the Universe.

Space Shuttle NASA's crewed rocket system that has been used since the early 1980s. The Shuttle consists of an Orbiter space plane, a huge fuel tank, and two rocket boosters.

Stage Part of a large rocket containing fuel and one or more rocket motors. When the fuel is used up, the stage falls away and another one takes over.

Survey To examine a territory to find out its physical features, such as distances between objects, and the height of its landforms.

▲ The U.S. Space Shuttle Orbiter, with its external fuel tank and boosters, one on each side.

◄ Useful scientific research is carried out aboard the International Space Station, which is in orbit around the Earth.

Index

Acknowledgements
We wish to thank all those people who
have helped to create this publication.
Information and images were supplied
by:
Individuals:
    Mat Irvine
    David Jefferis
NASA Sources:
    Don Davis
    John Frassanito & Associates
    Pat Rawlings (SAIC)
Organizations:
    Alpha Archive
    ESA European Space Agency
    iStockphoto:
        Penfold
        Sergey Korotkih
        P. Wei
    JPL Jet Propulsion Laboratory
    Marshall Image Xchange
    NASA Space Agency
    National Space Society
    Novosti News Agency
    The Artemis Project

Printed in the U.S.A.